LADY JUSTICE:

BLACK ANGEL'S REVENGE

BY

NANCY W. ROBINSON

Contents

Chapter One

I sat in the witness box looking at the Judge with a cool face... Everyone was expecting me to look afraid, anxious and fearful but the truth was that I wasn't bothered, I didn't care...
Everything was working according to my plans.
In my absent state of mind, I heard the judge saying ,"You Adebola Sandra popularly known as the black Angel has been found guilty of the following crimes
Robbery,
Sexual harassment,
Illegal drug activities
Bribery and corruption and finally the murder of her uncle Mr Harry Meghan...And is therefore sentenced to death by hanging.
COURT!!!! "
to everyone's surprise I burst into laughter, even the judge stared at me like I was mad
I kept on laughing for five minutes before I then said, "Ok... Ok.... Ok.. Agreed
I know I'm guilty but I'm not accepting my punishment "Immediately all the police pointed their guns at me.
Everyone knew I was a very dangerous lady... They knew what I was capable of doing, I laughed again and showed them my handcuffed hands...
"Come on,
Be realistic, There's nothing I can do with handcuffed hands... I'm a ki-ler not a magician...but let me tell you a story
It might take a while because it's a long story ,It's the story of my life.
I was born like any other child, I was born into a happy home as the first and only child,I had everything I wanted,I was happy.
But one day, the same day I celebrated my 10th year birthday, things went wrong for me. My world came crashing down I had the same "Name" Same "Face" but
A "DIFFERENT " ME!
Let me tell you my story,
The story of the "Black Angel "
But promise me... Promise me that you won't cry for me.

"Happy Birthday to you... Happy Birthday to you.. Happy birthday... Happy Birthday...Happy Birthday to you"
And then I cut the cake and everyone shouted "Hurrah"
I was beaming with Joy...
My dad was a successful businessman... He owned countless companies and had several shares with other companies. He was the third richest man in my country...in short, my dad was wealthy.
When it was the turn of uncle Harry whom I call uncle Harry, I so much loved him,
He was handsome,kind,and playful.
"Sorry baby, I ordered you something special but there was a delay in getting the delivery...it should be here this evening or tomorrow morning "
I was a bit sad "what's it uncle Harry"

He smiled and patted my cheeks. "A secret" I chuckled softly, Uncle Harry was fond of touching my body which I loved, I didn't see anything bad in it, I didn't even tell my parents.

At that moment, my dad's phone started ringing... He picked up the call and suddenly began to frown,I watched him whispering something into my mummy's Ear and my mom began to frown too,

Immediately, the party was canceled and everyone had to go home, but I noticed something strange. Uncle Harry was actually smiling....In my childish mind, I wondered why everyone was frowning and my uncle was smiling...I later got to know why.

After all the guests were gone, My daddy called me and hugged me tight,"Happy Birthday Sandry baby.... Sorry for disrupting your party, something came up at the company ,your mum and I have to go ,It's like we've been hacked by some fraudsters.

"Okay daddy.... "I said.

Mommy also hugged me and left with dad

It remained uncle Harry and I.

Normally, we all live together... Uncle Harry has his own apartment on the left wing of the duplex.

That night was the most unforgettable night of my life.

Later at night around midnight,dad and mum were yet to be home, I couldn't sleep because normally, either mum or dad had to pet me before I slept and there was nobody to pet me, then I remembered uncle Harry.

I climbed down from the bed and picked up my favorite pink teddy....Wore my baby slippers and walked out quietly to the left duplex wing. As I neared the apartment, something caught my attention, there was an odd smell, "Uncle Harry? " I called but no one answered me. I got scared and called again "Uncle Harry?

Are you there? "

As I was about to turn back, I heard uncle Harry's laughter,he was on the phone...I smiled and ran into the room,I was shocked.... Cigarettes were everywhere,

drinks which I later discovered were alcohol was everywhere... It was the cause of the weird smell.It was obvious that he was drunk and high but then I was too small and innocent to know.

"Uncle Harry!!!

What are you doing?" I shouted.

"I will report you to daddy and mummy,he looked at me slowly with red bloodshot eyes,I've never seen him looking like that before ,It was so strange and scary he started laughing crazily.

"Daddy?

Mummy?

Well they are no more I killed them"

My young heart skipped a bit...Killed my daddy and mummy?

"Why?" I quietly asked.

"Because I needed their properties,"he replied,``I became more confused."Why not ask for it? My daddy will give you "He laughed like a maniac again and moved slowly towards me with my heart beating fast like a rabbit's. I moved back slowly repeating the word.

"My mummy... My mummy.. My mummy"

He kept on walking towards me with an evil face, I didn't know what to do... I suddenly turned and ran towards the safety of my room....I was so terrified,

I didn't make it to the door before a smack landed on my back... It was so strange because nobody has ever hit Me, my parents never believed in corporal punishment.
I was so stunned that I couldn't shout, I only opened my mouth in a silent scream.
The sound never came out,he smacked me again.. Harder this time and I got my voice back I screamed on top of my lungs
He got more frustrated and hit me severally on my body. I was just screaming... For the first time in my life, I experienced pain
After a while, he shoved me up and pushed me into his apartment back I couldn't look into his face due to fear, I was just shivering and whimpering,he faced me and told me to kneel down,Instantly without disobeying, I complied and knelt down,"Do you like lollipops Sandra...?" he asked.
"Y.. Ye... Yes Uncle Harry..."
"Tell me Sandra,what do you do with lollipops". Something dropped from my lips and I saw that it was a drop of blood, my lips were busted...I felt all my back hurting me.
"I li.. Lick them "
"Good Girl" He said smiling ,"Now,
I'm going to give you a bigger and better lollipop and you're going to suck it"
I looked around but there was no sign of candies,I was thinking my uncle wanted to apologize to me for the beating so that I won't tell mummy and daddy.
I made up my childish mind to accept the sweet but still report him to my parent and then we would chase him out of our house
So I nodded my head and said,"Yes uncle"
He pulled an armchair and sat in front of me and pulled out his d**k.
I gasped and closed my eyes immediately,
I closed my eyes immediately... It was so embarrassing to me, "Un..Uncle....."I stammered,he slapped me with full force and I fell with blood splattering on the tiles....
He pulled my beautiful hairstyle with beads made specially for my birthday and dragged me to my knees,he slapped me again and told me to close my eyes and imagine that I was licking my usual lollipop, I obeyed and opened my mouth as he plunged his d**k into my throat.
I choked immediately, almost throwing up my dinner. He was obviously enjoying himself. I heard him making weird noises I've never heard in my entire life.
Suddenly I felt warmth in my throat, something hot and irritating was in my mouth,I couldn't bear it anymore. I threw up instantly and in exchange, I got another round of beating.
I didn't know when the pool of tears started pouring down my chubby cheeks deep in my mind, I wondered what I did wrong?
Why All these pains ?
Won't my parents come home?
Is it a bad dream?
More tears flowed down my cheeks and I burst out into tears,all my years had been a protective one built with love and cares,
It was all so strange,I felt so terrified...
"Un...Uncle Harry...
Un.. Un...Un... Uncleeeeee......
Pleaseeee stopppppp"

Chapter Two

For a moment, everything stopped... I guess even though he was touched by my tears, his face suddenly changed back to the familiar kind face I knew, "Oh my God!
My baby girl Sandra?
What have I done?
Are you okay? "
All my body was stained with blood
I could barely breathe,as he moved near me, I moved to the back still scared of him
His eyes were filled with fake tears but then I thought he was really sorry,I moved back but my head was spinning, I was feeling faint...The last thing I saw before I passed out was when he tried to hold my hand.
I opened my eyes feeling pains, my head and cheeks were still hurting, unconsciously tears began to pour down my eyes. My mind started remembering all what happened the day before and the next thought that came to my mind was
"My parents "
Yes, my parents... They promised to be back, they should be back by now, I quickly rose up from the bed and ran out into the adjoining room... My parent's room, to my utter surprise and shock
Nobody was there, the room was still neat like yesterday's night and the bed sheets were still laid. My heart started pounding furiously,i was scared then I remembered uncle Harry's statement,"I KILLED THEM "
Immediately, fear gripped my heart,
I quickly jumped onto my parents bed and curled up placing my thumb in my mouth, I stopped the bad habit of thumb sucking when I was 7 but all of a sudden, I needed something to comfort me,I closed my eyes wishing everything was a dream and that uncle Harry didn't hurt me, I wished I could forget but I couldn't I kept on remembering the pains, hurts and beatings,I remembered the way he forced me to suck his private part and I shivered again soon,
I started hearing footsteps coming towards the door, it was him... Uncle Harry.
"Sandra...? "He called
I heard but I was too terrified to reply,my lips were shaking.
"Sandra? " He called again and then slowly he opened the door. I closed my eyes and curled tighter but I was shaking. He entered the room and said,"I know you're awake, I didn't find you in your room so I knew you were here "
He moved nearer and spanked me on my ass,i cried out in pain and sat up, he laughed and said,"As from today henceforth I want you to remain obedient,
Whenever I call you and you don't reply... I will hurt you..Understand!!!? "
'Ye... Ye...Yess" I replied, shaking.
"Good Girl,
I expect them to bring me the news of your parent's death soon...I mustn't see you come downstairs... Okay? "

I nodded and he smiled. As soon enough, the doorbell rang,Uncle Harry stood up and went downstairs. Soon I heard him shout,"Jesusssssss.... What happened to them... ..My God!!!!
"Deep in my heart,
I knew that disaster had struck,I stood shivering in my room as I heard my uncle's shouts of fake sorrow,deep down inside my heart, I knew that things were going to change for me.
My heart started beating rapidly, I sat down on the floor beside my bedside and folded my knees and started crying.
"mommy... mommy " I said and started crying silently, I started wishing that everything was a bad dream.It was just too much for me to take,I just felt like I was going to die... were my parents really gone for good?
Did uncle Harry really kill them?
Was I really never going to see them again?
I remembered my parents cuddling me, reading bedtime stories for me, was everything going to end......?
These were the thoughts of my mind till I fell asleep. I woke up with a tap on my shoulder.It was my uncle. I gasped and moved back in shock.He smiled gently but my heart kept beating furiously. I started shaking again.
He touched my face tenderly but the expression on his face was that of evil
He looked like he wanted to eat me up
"Come and bathe,,....after that you will eat and then we will discuss
Is that clear? "
I was too scared to speak, I only nodded quickly.
He smiled and pulled me up, all I wanted was to run away from him but I knew that would earn me another beating so I followed him gently as he led me to my private bathroom,"Sandra remove your clothes "Reluctantly I took them off... I saw him looking at my fast growing breast with an evil expression,"Climb into that tub "..he ordered, I did so but my mind was at unease, What was Uncle Harry's plan for me with my shaky legs I obeyed.
I climbed gently into the tub wondering what was his next plan for me,but I had learnt a very good lesson, disobedience would earn me a through beating....So as to avoid it, I must learn to be obedient
So I stood in the tub without complaining, he filled the tub with warm water and started bathing my body.
He took his time to embarrass and do naughty things to my body. First, he started with my tiny immature nipples. He played a bit with it, twisting and turning it. I closed my eyes, irritated. I felt like screaming but I tried my best to hide it.
But my lips were already shaking...Uncle Harry started drawing lines with his index finger on my body "Hmmmm... Sandra
I'm gonna keep you as my personal toy... You're gonna learn a lot, In fact you have a lot to learn, how to please me, how to make me happy,as long as you do so, you're safe and won't end up like your parents... Is it clear?
"Ye.. Yes uncle Harry" I said shivering.
"That's my girl" he said with a smile
Now come and eat... I sat down naked to eat because he instructed me not to wear any clothing. The food set was my favorite meal, Fried rice and jollof with chicken and beef and fried

plantains... Normally I was supposed to be glad but it brought only memories of my mother. My eyes filled instantly with tears but I sniffed them in... Everything was so strange and scary to me.I was just 10 years old and I woke up one morning to see that my parents were gone and I was an orphan. Here I was cold and naked in front of my favorite uncle who claimed to have killed them.Fear filled my heart and soul, nothing made sense... It was like a bad dream as I stared at my food, Uncle Harry barked at me.
"EAT UP IDIOT!!!"
The word stung me like a slap...I had never been called an idiot in my life before all I experienced was pampering and excess love.
I picked up my spoon and started stuffing my mouth with food. The food was nice but then it tasted like rubber in my mouth.... I was eating out of fear and not out of hunger......After forcefully filling my stomach, Uncle Harry grabbed me and pulled me into his room. He carried me and dumped me on his bed without care. I bounced back and moved quietly to the last edge of the bed. He locked the door and started undressing, I averted his glare and looked away, My heart was beating very fast,i was thinking he was going to make me suck his d**k like the previous day but he had more plans for me.... Evil plans.
After stripping naked, he climbed into the bed with me and pulled me closer to his side,Then he kissed me voraciously.. Like an animal... like a beast..i tried to push him off but his weight was something else.
He kissed all my face...my neck.. My nipples... All these while, I was screaming.... I didn't know why but I was so scared... I knew it wasn't going to end well for me, when my shouts got too loud... He got up and gave me a hot beating....After that he pulled a box under his wardrobe and removed ropes and handcuffs, I was surprised... What was he going to do? He pulled me and cuffed my hands together and tied my legs separately with ropes to the bed posts.
I hope you all understand my position... I was laying on my back with my legs spread apart wide and my hands were cuffed together over my head...i was practically helpless,Then to make matters worse,he covered my mouth tightly with a piece of cloth my screams couldn't come out loud like before again...sweats was pouring down my face and neck despite the air conditioner in the room the only thing I could do was to shake my head, I was shaking it vehemently with water pouring from my eyes Uncle Harry was so heartless, he turned deaf eyes to my pleas and thrust himself deep into my little young vulnerable body, I screamed.... The pain was unbearable... I felt a warm liquid slipping out from my body... Then I was too young to know what it was... All I knew was that uncle Harry was hurting me and he was doing it badly......Was I going to survive this?
Was I going to live?
I looked at the ceiling and the last thought in my mind was "Mommy... Daddy... Where are you? "

Chapter Three

(Three weeks later)
It was confirmed that my parents died in a motor accident due to brake failure. At first, my mother was in a coma for two weeks before she finally gave up the ghost... My dad died on the spot. All my parent's property was given to me but was to be managed by my guidance until I was 18 years old.
Unfortunately for me, Uncle y was my guidance... Everyone was deceived by the way he cried and wept at my parent's burial except me,I hated him... He disgusted me,I had no one to report him to so I only had to shut up.
Back home, the abuse continued unabated
Uncle Harry abused Me physically and sexually.... He turned me into a sex slave... At the age of twelve.. I was perfect at doing a blowjob and I could fuck properly.
To me, sex was just an act... A thing I did just to get away from punishment,I changed for the worse, I became reserved... I hated everyone including myself,I was no longer the chubby beautiful outspoken brilliant and funny Sandra everyone knew me as...i became distant.. Cold and dull... I rarely talked
I rarely smiled... I only stared at everyone with cold dark eyes... I was now used to the beatings and pains.
I took everything without complaining.
Sexual abuse does two things to its victims
It's either it shuts you down or shut you up
When it shuts you down, you become slow witted... You start behaving like a moron…
you start thinking slowly and become timid and easily scared,It brings forth the rabbit in you...
Your tame gentle part that's the broken down aspect of sexual assault.
But the other one that can happen to you is when you shut up you become quiet and cold as ice. It brings forth the demon in you.. You become a beast as well... You become heartless and cruel like attacker
Your thoughts are only filled with impure thoughts like killing and causing damage
You feel like shedding blood... You feel like making someone cry all you want is horror and chaos.
As for me, it brought forth the demon in me
It brought forth my dark side... You can call it the black me,I started having evil thoughts from the age of 15 about killing,
About shedding blood and mostly about killing my uncle, not just a mercy killing.
A painful slow death... That's all I wanted
I knew I needed a psychiatrist..but that was the least... The only thing to calm down my tumor was if I killed my molester
I knew that I had to kill him.
But things changed,Uncle Harry decided to marry.... That plan disrupted my plans a bit
He married a young lady called Margaret popularly known as Meggie. She was a young bright lady with great manners,
I hated Meggie but she made it impossible for me to hate her. She loved and cared for me even when I shoved her off and insulted her. She took it all with a smile and never got angry, her

patience and understanding was so strange, she behaved like an angel,she loved and treated me like her daughter... I started growing affections for her.

We got close and I noticed that uncle Harry was not comfortable with it... The affection that his wife had for me was genuine, many times she prevented him from beating me up... I never told her that her husband use to abuse me sexually... She didn't know anything.

All she knew was that my uncle was too harsh on me and she hated it... Soon,he started showing his real color to Meggie,he started beating her up too.

Many times... Whenever he wanted to beat me She would jump over me and cover me with her body and receive the beating instead of me...Sometimes when I see her husband beating her up,I will run and cover her with my own body and take the beating for her.

After that, we would treat each other's wounds with iodine and then laugh together like nothing's wrong... This created a bond between us. I loved her and she loved me as well...As for her,the abuse brought out her own timid part... It brought forth the rabbit in her.. She became scared of my uncle.

One day, I decided to tell her the truth...

I revealed it all to her, Meggie's reaction was so touching.... She didn't cry out loud but tears of pain dropped down her eyes....

Tears kept on rolling down until I gave her a handkerchief.

She looked at me slowly with red bloodshot eyes and said quietly,"I knew something was wrong with him from the first day my mother introduced him to me as my husband-to-be.

He looked somehow cool but underneath him... I sensed a cruel evil beast.... "She grabbed my hands,"Sandra... Please let's run away.... Let's leave him and escape... I have enough money for us to start a new life, I'm scared of him... Someone that could kill his own sister and her husband for money.... He's dangerous.

We would travel abroad.... And start all over again... Please " she said crying again, I smiled and held her hand back

"No Meggie... I don't care whether he kills me or not... All I need is revenge... For what he did to my family... My parents... Me... If I don't take something out of him... I won't survive.... Guilt and Anger will kill me.

If you're scared... You're free to leave Me.... Run away "She shakes her head and holds me back "No... I can't leave you

I will never leave you Sandra.. We're in this together.... I'm not going"

Water pulled into my eyes as I saw the affection she displayed.... That very day... I fell in love with Meggie... Not a s*xual love but an Agape love... Love that was warm and real...the kind of love I had for my parents.... I loved Meggie.

Things transformed in the house that day,

Meggie changed to something else... Even I myself was amazed.... I guess my story changed her... She stopped being timid like a rabbit...she became violent and harsh towards her husband.... She took everything for anger.... Small issues became something else...she became more protective of me.... Watching me like a hawk all the time..... Normally, she always travels abroad from time to time for shopping... But since I told her that my uncle uses that opportunity to molest me for weeks,she changed her perspectives... She stopped traveling at all. She stayed at home all the time and only went out when I was at school..... Anytime I felt sick, she was always home beside me,... It felt like I had another mother.

All these made uncle Harry aggressive... He couldn't touch me for months and I was getting better...My dullness started reducing.... I started feeling like a human being again but things were worse for uncle Harry.... His s*x slave wasn't available for him anymore.... His wife wasn't traveling anymore and anytime she wanted to... She took me along so it was impossible for him to have me

All these things happened to me when I was 17 years old.... The unexpected happened the day I wrote my last paper.... I was 17 years old... Almost 18 when I was in grade 12....After signing out and as everyone else was tearing their clothes... Taking pictures...having fun... I walked to the back of the school to sit,I wasn't a fan of fun anymore... I didn't celebrate anything... Not even my birthday because that was the same day I lost my parents so I avoided anything called Fun or celebration because it brought back bad memories of my life.....Most of my mates thought I was proud and mannerless because I rarely talked nor played.

I was always looking blank...my face was void of any emotions and I grew up to be a very beautiful girl.... I was that kind of girl that attracts people to herself both males and females but I was damn cold and annoying... I built a thick wall of coldness around myself that kept people off the bay.... It made people stay off me because I was always cold and harsh...

Another behavior I had was to always smile at insults.... It was always cold.... Evil smile.... No matter what you say to me, I would just smile and look at you with cold chilling eyes till you finally look away....this attitude made many avoid me and it made me happy because I always wanted to be left alone....anytime I was alone... I was happy... I felt free from my problems... I hated being around people.

So when I went to the back of the school to sit down, nobody called me and those that went passed me left me alone.... They didn't bother disturbing me.... I was lost in thought enjoying my solitude until someone tapped me on my shoulders....

I looked up slowly with Cold Eyes to attack my disturber only to find Meggie smiling at me.... I was shocked and surprised.

"Meggie! " I said, smiling a little bit more warmly.... "You're here?... What are you doing here? "...I asked.

She smiled back stiffly to me and said

"I came to pick you up to celebrate your passing out of college...i knew you would be alone " she said trying to smile but something told me that something was wrong.

Meggie was acting strange.... I wondered what was wrong as I packed my books into my bag and went to join her in her car.

We got home in thirty minutes after doing a little shopping....I kept on asking Meggie if she was fine and she said "Of course darling.. I'm fine.

As we entered the house... I showered and changed my dress to something more comfortable...

As I walked to the dining, I saw that Meggie was already setting the table gently and was placing my favorite food,Jollof and fried rice with chicken and beef with fried plantains.... If you remember clearly... Although I loved this meal, it brought forth memories of my dead mother who was always spoiling me with the treat of jollof and fried rice.... I wished she was alive to see me passing out of secondary school and water filled my eyes but I quickly swallowed it back... I couldn't cry...it was a promise I made to myself.

As I sat down... I grabbed Meggie's hand and said, smiling at her, "Thanks Meggie... You gave me another chance to live.

Chapter Four

instantly water filled Meggie's eyes and started pouring down with shaky lips she said.
"I'm... I'm... I'm so sorry Sandra....
I... I... Wa... Was weak... He threatened to kill my parents...I've let you down Sandra "
My heart started racing,"What did you do Meggie...? " I asked..."What did he make you do" I asked urgently again... Grabbing her hands....
"He... He... He... Made me poison you.. I've poisoned your food "
The spoon dropped off my hands....
"What"!!! I said I felt terrified... Meggie looked so sad and bad.
"He has my parents kidnapped and he has promised to kill them if I don't cooperate.... He said once you're 18,...all the companies shall be yours and he's not ready to give them up, the only way to save my parents is if I agree to kill you...."
I stood up and ran to the corner of the dinning, obviously shaking.
"So what will you do now.... Will you kill me? " I asked, feeling scared.
More tears flowed from Meggie's eyes as she shook her head left and right....
"No darling.. I don't think I can... I'm sorry for being a coward... If you die... Nobody will stop that animal and he would do more evil...Now run to you room and pack all your valuable stuffs and come back here"
I did as she told me and dashed into my room,packed some of my clothes and my diary and then I picked up a family album of My dead parents and I then came back to meet her still standing at the table ...
She smiled and gave me a picture that both of us took together and gave Me her favorite pendant necklace...
She opened her purse and removed her two Atm cards and gave them to me
"I have five hundred thousand in each card... Withdraw it all before it gets blocked "
She gave me her car keys since I already learnt how to drive and then she placed 350k cash into my palm... It was a huge amount of money.
I was astonished... Then we hugged one last time... It was a tight hug....
We both started crying at the painful departure.....After the hug...Meggie kissed my forehead and said,"I love you Sandra"
"I love you Meggie..." I replied
"What about your parents...? " I asked, getting worried...
She smiled and said,"I'm a coward... I can't fight for them"
Then before I knew what was happening... Meggie carried the food I was supposed to eat and ate over 8 spoons.
I screamed "NOOOOOOOOOOOOOOO!!!! "
But I couldn't stop her.... Meggie had already swallowed the poisoned food...in 30 seconds.. The poison started reacting... I tried carrying her to the hospital but Meggie shakes her head smiling...
She was already coughing and was finding it difficult to breathe,he was already on the floor kneeling... I tried pulling her up but she grabbed my hand weakly and said
"Sandra.... This... This... This isn't your fault.... It's.. It's the only way to pro... Pro...protect you.

Throw away your phone and start all over again....Run away from here and return only when you're strong enough to face that beast.... " she started coughing blood

"Even if you take me to the hospital... I won't survive this because it's a very deadly poison...it has no cure.... Soon I will be dead...

Now escape before he returns home... I've written a suicide note and I've done a short video on how I killed myself... I did it to protect you because I know that he can frame you up for my death... I lied in my video that I was going to kill myself due to depression....only you and I know the real truth.... When you went upstairs to pack your bags... I posted it... Soon... Your uncle will be rushing here so you need to escape Sandra... But remember....it was your uncle that did all this.... He killed your parents and abused you...

Kidnapped my parents and he's the cause of my death.... Make... Make him pay Sandra... Make him pay" she said and died in my arms... Smiling.

Meggie died smiling.

I couldn't believe it.... Meggie died to save me... I started shaking her vigorously...

"Meggie... No... No.. No... Meggie... Please don't die... Don't leave me.... Please don't die... Meggie, wake up.... Meggie... You're my only friend... Please Meggie... I can't deal with this... Meggie please " I said weeping uncontrollably....it was too much for me to bear....

My parents had died but I didn't see it happen but Meggie's death was different... It shocked me,It moved me....

I understood why she had killed herself, if she ran away with me, my uncle would keep on threatening her with her parents whom he had kidnapped.....

As tears continued dropping from my eyes massively..... I knew that things would never be the same again before my uncle came back home, I quickly picked up all my stuff and with a heavy heart I kissed Meggie's forehead and promised to take revenge at all costs.

In my mind's eye, I imagined Meggie smiling at me... Who said Meggie was weak... Who said she was a coward... She wasn't... She was the one that made me realize how evil uncle Harry was.

"To overcome such an evil... A greater evil needs to be required"

And that greater evil was me.... Sandra....The angel that brought death

THE BLACK ANGEL.

TWO YEARS LATER

People yelled

"You can do it Angel... You can.... Come on!!!!.... Fight

Fight !!

Fight!!"

I couldn't take the blows anymore... I raised my left hand and screamed "I give up!!! "Justin left me and smiled "Maybe next time Angel.... I smiled back and allowed him to pull me up...my lips were bursted and I knew that one of my fingers was broken but I was used to it... I was becoming tough but not really tough.

Now to explain how I got to where I was is a long story entirely but let me make it as short as possible....after Meggie's death and my absconding from home.

My uncle raised a false alarm that I was kidnapped and the kidnappers asked for a big ransom which he paid and still I was yet to be released... The police got involved and I was being searched for.... Nobody knew that I was running for my own life.... I knew that the whole society was seeing him as a pitiful person... Everyone was pitying him.... His lovely pregnant wife just committed suicide due to depression and still uploaded the video before killing herself and his darling cousin was missing.

Everyone was sorry for him..... Except me of course... I knew the truth and somebody else,all these while.... There was somebody watching me.....someone I knew not, I escaped to Italy two weeks after Meggie's death and he followed me secretly making sure that the police never found me.

Then one day, he showed up in front of my hotel door.I thought it was just the room service until he said.

"How long will you run away from your destiny Sandra"

I tried to close the door back but he had slipped in like an eel unexpectedly....

"Who are you? " I asked with a shaky voice.

"A lover of Justice " he replied with a smile

Then he sat me down and informed me that he was the assassin hired by Uncle Harry to kill my parents....so in short... He killed my parents,My hand started shaking

"Will you kill me too" I said obviously afraid

He laughed... "If I wanted you dead... You won't be speaking by now.

"so... What do you want...? " I asked him

"After I killed your parents.... Your uncle promised me 50 million Naira which he gave me before the Job and then after the Job... He made plans to kill me which I almost died from.... But as an experienced Assassin I've been on the run for a while and I've been monitoring you for over seven years....

Your Uncle is so Evil....

And sometimes to overcome a great Evil.... You need a greater evil. Sandra, are you ready to avenge all your family's death? He asked.

"Yes please " I replied with a shaky voice

He took all the money I had on me and started training me... I became damned good at guns and knives...

Martial Arts and crafts.... I even went into using poisons to kill, I went into drugs and alcohol and after training for a year I was better than him.... He called me one evening and handed me a short note describing a hidden academy for Assassins..... He then said,

"Angel... Do you remember what I told you a year ago"I removed the cigarette I was puffing on slowly from my mouth and said

"Yes I remember... "He smiled and said "Prove it"

What I did next showed how heartless I was....I removed my gun with swift accuracy and shot him Dead!

He was so shocked as he fell to the ground... Dying slowly.

I moved to his side and repeated the same slogan he taught me.

"To overcome a great Evil, A greater Evil is needed.

I did that for my parents.It was my first kill and I enjoyed it so much...I took the address...

Packed my stuff... Found my way to the academy which was located in the desert....it admits only 75 students per every three years but only 5 graduates.... The remaining 70 died,I registered and here I am.

Chapter Five

I sat down nursing my broken finger after the fight...then someone threw a clean towel at me... I looked up and saw him... Justin.

He nodded without smiling and turned away....Justin was the number one top fighter that deals with killing with just breaking of bones and spinal cords.

He was also good at shooting from a far range....He was a very great sniper... He was handsome and Wicked... He fights without mercy during training...Remember I said that out of 75 students only 5 survive.....We remain only 50...25 had died during training and Justin had killed 10 himself during the training... Many feared him.

He was one of the most likely assassins to graduate alive...he was a Spanish and I guessed his age should be around the range of 25 or 30...he didn't mind who his opponent was... Male or female...

Handsome or beautiful or Ugly...Sick or Healthy...he would definitely fight with the person like he was fighting with his deadly enemies.

In the Academy... Nobody makes friends...everyone is someone else's enemy, so I was surprised to see Justin throwing a towel at me...I looked closer at the towel before using it to clean my sweat for the fear that Justin might have placed poison on him....

Unknown to me, Justin was busy looking at me from a distance... Smiling at me.

" Balance your feet Angel!!!....Balance it... Yes.. Yes... Now lift your right arm in a curved form and swing... Yes babe... You're doing well... That's the shing tan Zü... Also known as......speaking the Korean language fluently....Justin wasn't only good at fighting.. He could speak 36 foreign languages and write them properly as well.

One way we became friends....it was ridiculous and strange but we kept it a secret...we had a secret hideout where he trained me specially and started teaching me all sorts of Martial Arts...In 3 months I was already matching him because I learnt very fast and Justin was a great teacher...he was better than most of our trainers.

He never asked me about my life story and I never told him mine as well nor did I ask him.

To cut the long story short...

We started developing feelings for one another. This fateful day after training... As I was packing my bag... Justin came behind me and pulled me up and started kissing me with high passion....At first, I was still... I had never had a proper sex before and it felt all strange... I became scared of moving and it seemed like Justin understood me...he hugged me tightly and said,"With time babe.. One day at a time "

So everyday after secret training.. He would pull me into his arms and kiss me tenderly.It went on for weeks until one day I responded to the kiss.

I opened up my mouth and lips and kissed him back slowly and shyly.It was my first normal kiss...I took my time... Kissing and exploring his lips.

He pushed me to the wall and started exploring my body, starting from my neck... He kissed a particular spot on my throat that made me shiver. Placing his two hands on my boobs and started giving it a gentle squeeze....I moaned a bit as Justin tore open my shirt... Removed my boobs and started playing with my nipples... Rubbing them in between his fingers... The feeling was so cool..."Hmmmmm" I said...

He kissed me again and continued undressing me... Soon I was naked in his arms and he was naked too.

He pushed me flat down on the floor and spread my laps but the moment he did so... My psychological problem slots in... In my mind's eye... I saw Justin as uncle Harry trying to rape me again...

I tried my best to convince my brain that I was hallucinating... I was seeing the wrong thing...My heart knew I was seeing Justin but my brain was seeing something else.

Tears of frustration started dropping from my eyes... I knew I was going to do something wrong, I tried warning him.

""Just... Justin... I... I... Please... Please stop... " but he couldn't listen... He didn't .

What I did next was so unexpected of me... I raised my hands and started slapping him rapidly....it seemed like a joke to him at first... But soon I started attacking him with all my strength.... My brain was already seeing him as someone else... I started growling like a maniac,"Uncle Harry... This is your end.

I will deal with you for everything you have done to me and my parents and most importantly to Meggie..."

I was saying all this with a cruel voice and was squeezing Justin's neck.....Distantly I was hearing Justin's voice "Angel... Angel... Angel... Stop this... You're hallucinating... I'm not him.. " but I didn't listen... When Justin saw that I wasn't ready to listen and was hurting him badly... He took a stone beside him and hit me on my head till I became unconscious.

I woke up with a splitting headache... All my head was on fire... My tongue was burning.

As I tried to raise my body... My head started spinning around and I almost fainted again...."Don't move.. It will only become worse... " I heard a familiar voice saying... The voice showed and I saw Justin with a cup of an unknown drink with him. I tried remembering what happened but I couldn't... All I remembered was the kiss.

He passed me the drink and said,"Take that...it would help..."He knelt down beside me and made me drink a bit....After a while... I asked.

"What happened to me ..?

Did we have sex? "

Justin looked at me with funny eyes

"Sex....???

Wait... You didn't remember? "

I nodded and said,"Nope...i didn't"

He smiled for the first time and I couldn't help myself....he looked so handsome.

"Who's Uncle Harry Angel?...He asked, looking calm and soft,"Is he the reason why you're here?"

I knew that I had done something terrible... Then I noticed scratches all over his face...

He had a small cut on his forehead as well..."Wait... " I said gently...

"Who did that?...it wasn't there when we were training ,did I do that? "

He smiled again and said, "You almost killed me Angel.

I think you need a psychiatrist....you're hallucinating...you took me for that uncle Harry of yours"

Water filled my eyes again... I hid my face in shame but Justin gave a small chuckle and said "Babe...

I'm not a psychiatrist but let me tell you this

For you to get healed... You will need to get out of this place alive...
Then you must settle this score you have with that man only then will you be finally free....:No
amount of therapy or drugs will change you....until you fulfill your heart desire....
Do you know what your heart desires?" He asked...
"Yes..." I replied softly...
'My heart desire is to kill him slowly and painfully... I want to see him crawl and beg for mercy... I
want to see him suffer and then kill him in the worst way ever, only then will I be okay.
Help me Justin... Will you please help me? " I said, gripping his hands with tears pouring down
my cheeks.
He held me back and said, "On one condition..."
"What is that? " I asked.
" After fulfilling your goal.... You must marry me"
I laughed thinking he was joking but when I saw that he wasn't smiling I asked.
"Are you serious..? "
He nodded.
"Will you marry me Angel..? "
I smiled and said "I'm sorry I can't "
"I will wait for you, " he said.
"Don't wait...I won't be there" I replied.
"I love you Angel"
"Justin... I'm not made for love...I've been ruined for that and everyone I had ever loved died...
Mom... Dad... Meggie... I can't let you join the league even now. I'm not capable of loving
anymore.
I have no feelings... The only feeling I have is the hatred I feel towards Uncle Harry....
Even if it takes killing you to fulfill my destiny, I will kill you.
Then I stood up weakly and left him... Hiding my face so that he doesn't see the tears pouring.
We didn't stop training but Justin never brought it up again nor did he touch me...
He trained me until I almost matched his strength.
Sometimes I felt like running into his arms...Sometimes I just wanted to forget my past and
escape with him to another country and start all over again.
But the thirst and cravings for revenge didn't allow me.
I pushed all the emotions back away and faced my training.
Soon my three year training lapsed and the examinations began, we started as 75
But at the beginning of the exams... We were 28....Definitely.. 23 students had to die.
The first round was simple... The three best students were picked and separated from the rest.
The best two were Justin, Xi Chang (A Chinese guy).
Remember we were 28 in all but the obvious two best were picked out of the rest of us making it
26 students left.
During the first week of our exams....
Justin and Xi Chang were picked to fight on Wednesday in the cell with all the students
watching. In my heart... I feared for Justin because everyone knew how brutal and beastly Xi
Chang could be...
On Tuesday evening... During my training with Justin.. I was moody, he noticed this and asked.
"Angel... Are you okay....? "

Chapter Six

I looked up at his handsome flawless face and suddenly wanted to cry... What if Justin dies...?
How will I survive the exams....he had been my source of inspiration, Justin looked so worried
for me... He wasn't even bothered about himself.
"'Jus..Justin.. " I stammered.
"What if you don't make it tomorrow...?
What If you die...?
What if you're not able to make it...? "
He smiled and shrugged saying
"Do I have a choice...? "
Without thinking I blurted out my mind
"Let's run away Justin... Let's escape
Let's go and start all over... I'm scared ...I don't want to lose you.
Every single person I loved died and left me, My dad..My mom...Meggie... One way or the
other,they died... And I don't want the same thing befalling you.
Please let's run away...."
At first he was emotionless... Then suddenly he smiled one of his rare smiles then walked gently
toward me and hugged me tight.
I wrapped my arms around his neck and buried my face in his neck inhaling his familiar smell.
Praying deeply to God that I mustn't lose Justin again..... I felt a warm liquid slipping on my neck
and I knew that he was also crying like me.
"Ang... Ang.. Angel....
I'm scared.. I'm so scared about tomorrow
I mustn't die... I know that I mustn't...i want to be there for you ..i want to help you take your
revenge and then propose properly to you and start a sweet life afresh with you
Angel... I don't want to leave you"
I hugged him tightly and started crying with him.
That was the last day in my life that I sobbed really bitterly for almost an hour.. I never cried that
much anymore In my life
Justin released me after a while and wiped my tears away from my cheeks using his thumbs...
I raised my thumbs and cleaned his face using the same method. Then he looked deeply into
my eyes and said, "You know we can't run away Angel...
I can't run neither can you... We must do it or die...if we try escaping we will definitely be dead.
Remember we're in the middle of the desert...we were all blind folded and placed in a helicopter
to this place.
We don't know the exact place we are... We don't know how to escape... Nor do we have a
map... So the only way to get out of this place alive is to fight.
We must be heartless like assassins... We must learn to kill brutally... So we must be brutal.
If I fight and win this fight... I won't have to fight with you anymore... Automatically I've been
chosen. So I'm not only fighting for my life... I'm fighting for you... For your revenge and for our
future...
So I will fight Angel.... I will fight till my last breath.."

I cupped his cheeks with my hands... Raised myself on my toes and kissed him passionately with tears dripping down my eyes.

I couldn't sleep throughout that night... After placing countless acupuncture Needles into both my body and Justin's... I still couldn't feel at rest.

I was the first person to arrive at the cell the second day.. Even before the fight started.

The only good thing about the fight was that the winner will be automatically picked and will be given a gift of 5 million dollars

Then he's to work for the agency alone for a year before he will be given independence.

While the remaining four will be given 1 million dollars each with also a work permit with the agency for only 6 months.

So if Justin wins this fight...i won't have any fear of fighting with him but the worst part is that someone must die.

The fight began soon and both parties were proving strong.

After two hours they were both sweating profusely,they exchanged blows and punches and went into martial arts...

It was so obvious that both of them were very strong and nobody was ready to surrender...

Then the sword fight was introduced lastly... I got scared a bit.

Everyone knew that Xi Chang was a very dangerous sword fighter. Soon he tore Justin's Arm and my heart started aching

After thirty minutes... It was so obvious that Xi Chang was gaining upper hand then all of a sudden... Justin made a very smart move and knocked the sword off Chang's hands... I screamed out for joy...but to my uttermost shock.

Chang charged like a monkey and tore Justin's eyes with his long fingernails like magic.It was so shocking to everyone because Chang did it with the speed of lighting.

Justin dropped his sword and held his eyes... His left eye was badly affected.... It was bleeding... Temporary Justin was rendered blind.

I couldn't cry out but my heart was so heavy....it was so obvious that Justin would be killed.. he can't see.

Justin soon had blood all over him from the stabs from Chang's swords.

As Chang raised his sword to give him his final stab... Justin miraculously gripped the sword with his hands.... He was already Lying on the floor but I didn't know where he got the supernatural strength from.

He gripped the sharp edgy part and used it to stand. Immediately I recognized the style Justin was using.

He was using the unknown shing tan Zü..... the unknown and most dangerous Korean style of fighting... only few knew it and only fewer could master it.

With closed eyes.. Justin rose up and side tracked Chang and with few moves without giving him a chance.... He broke Chang's spinal cord by only using his index finger curved to hit that straight cord behind his neck.. Breaking that small bone and snapping out his life,Chang fell lifeless and Justin fell beside him also unconscious.

The judges opened the cell where the two were fighting to check who was still alive as they neared Chang...it was obvious that he was dead.

Justin was checked and he was still breathing... Instantly he was rushed out for medical treatment..All his face was bloody and messy.

I wondered if he was ever going to see again with those eyes... As he was carried out..he did something very amazing.
He raised his right hand high and gave me this sign.
Water filled my eyes... Justin just told me that he would survive and he's waiting for me to survive as well.
My Justin was gonna live...he just showed me that he will never give up...so must I..
I closed my eyes and smiled.
I was going to win this exam.. Get out of here alive and survive.
I never got to see Justin again until the day we were to finally pass out of the training school.
The rest of us went through a different type of examination,remember that the rest of us were 24.
The following day.. A jet arrived and we were all asked to enter...we were asked not to take anything.
As we all settled down, a flat screen popped up and we heard a female voice saying.
WELCOME ON BOARD MY FELLOW CRIMINALS...
THIS IS YOUR FINAL TEST AND FOR YOU TO PASS THIS TEST EXCELLENTLY
YOUR ABILITIES MUST BE TESTED PROPERLY
YOUR SMARTNESS
YOUR AGILITY
YOUR EFFECTIVENESS
YOUR WICKEDNESS
YOUR BRUTALITY
YOUR BEAST
THE DEMON IN YOU MUST TAKE CHARGE
YOUR MISSION HERE IS ARRIVE ON A DESERTED FOREST FILLED WITH ALL SORTS OF DANGEROUS THINGS
YOU'RE WEAPONLESS
YOU HAVE NO CLOTHES
YOU HAVE NO FOOD
YOU HAVE NO FRIENDS
YOU HAVE NO COMPANION
BUT YOU CAN SURVIVE...I KNOW YOU'RE SAYING THAT'S IT'S IMPOSSIBLE
BUT I'M TELLING YOU THAT IT'S POSSIBLE
BECAUSE I SURVIVED AND I'M ONE OF THE MOST WANTED CRIMINAL IN THE WORLD
YET NEITHER THE COPS NOR THE FBI COULD GET ME
I'M SMARTER THAN ALL OF THEM
SO YOU'RE ALL GONNA PASS THROUGH THESE TO BECOME SOMEONE LIKE ME
I STILL KILL TILL TODAY
THERE'S NO ONE I CAN'T KILL... EVEN THE PRESIDENT OF USA ISN'T SAFE
AND YET I'VE NEVER BEEN CAUGHT...
THE ONLY WAY I CAN GET CAUGHT IS IF I WILLINGLY SURRENDER
SOON YOU WILL BECOME SOMEONE LIKE ME
NOW BACK TO YOUR MISSION
YOU'RE GOING TO BE ON A DESERTED FOREST

Chapter Seven

YOUR MISSION IS TO MAKE IT TO A BUILDING ON THE HILL
INSIDE THAT BUILDING, YOU WILL FIND 4 TUBES
ONCE YOU GET THE TUBE... YOU WILL KNOW WHAT TO DO
YOU MUSTN'T TAKE MORE THAN ONE TUBE... IF YOU DO... YOU AUTOMATICALLY
EXPLODE
AND OOPS... IF YOU LOOK OUT OF THE WINDOW
YOU WILL FIND OUT THAT WE HAVE REACHED OUR DESTINATION
WE'RE IN THE MIDDLE OF NOWHERE......(The voice laughed mischievously)
WERE YOU EXPECTING THE JET TO LAND PROPERLY?.... OH NO... I'M SORRY
YOU WILL HAVE TO JUMP OUT....YOU WILL HAVE TO LOOK FOR THE PARACHUTES IN
BAGS... INSIDE THE BAGS ARE FEW THINGS YOU WILL NEED
AND I FORGOT TO TELL YOU THIS......THERE'S A BOMB IN THIS JET... IN THE NEXT FIVE
MINUTES... THE JET IS EXPLODING... THE PILOT MUST HAVE PLACED THE JET IN A
AUTO DRIVE MODE...HE MUST HAVE ESCAPED FROM THE PLANE
AND THE FINAL GIST IS THAT YOU GUYS ARE 26 RIGHT?
THERE ARE ONLY 15 BAGS...SO ONLY 15 PEOPLE ARE GOING TO ESCAPE FROM THIS
PLANE ALIVE... THE REST ARE GOING TO DIE...
YOUR TIME STARTS NOW... THANKS.
Immediately there was a great commotion in the plane... Everybody started running up and
down... We could all hear bomb timer.
FIVE FUCKING MINUTES!!!!!!
Everyone was panicking, including me... I wanted to join in the rush then I remembered Justin's
Words.
"IN TIME OF CRISIS BE CALM"
I tried to remain calm...I closed my eyes and took five deep breaths.
Then I bent down and placed my hand under the chair... I felt something hard and I pulled it
out... Behold it was a parachute bag.
I pulled my second seat and found another one ..in my calm state of mind.
I got two bags... I looked around and saw a small pretty lady looking very scared and was visibly
shaking.
"Hey!" I called ...she looked sharply to my side and I threw a bag to her and said
"Be fast!"
I wore mine as fast as possible and jumped out of the plane without waiting for anyone else.
After a while I was on the ground... I stood up and looked around.. Everywhere looked
deserted... It was like I was in the middle of nowhere.
I sighed loudly... Prayed to God that I survived everything that was going to happen in this
deserted place.
I opened my bag and found two guns fully loaded with bullets... I saw two Jack knives,
A disposable lamp and a Touch light.
I found small cans of fruits and food enough to last me a few days only.
And I found a yellow map placed with a compass.. At the end of the map was a building... I
guessed that was the building I was expected to enter.

As I started packing up my stuff to start my journey... I heard a soft footstep behind me
Quickly using my instincts... I turned around and cocked my gun.. Ready to blow whosoever
head it was.
It turned out to be the timid lady I rescued earlier... She was smiling sheepishly...
I didn't return her smile... I had no time for useless pleasantries...I turned back and continued
tracing my way with the map in my hands.
"Hi.. " she said.
I didn't reply.
"I'm Fiona.. "
I didn't reply.
"I wanted to say Thank you for saving my life earlier.. "
I didn't reply
"I'm grateful.. "
I didn't reply.
"Can we be friends... It's been a long time since I had a friend.. I mean someone to talk to.. "
I didn't reply...
"I really want us to be friends.."
I was already getting frustrated.. This lady was nothing else but a parrot.
I stopped my tracks and faced her with the hardest face I could make and said slowly
" I do not need friends.
And if you want us to walk together, be Quiet!!!!
I said it so harshly that I expected her to freak out or become scared and shut up but instead
she smiled widely... She looked so beautiful when smiling.
"So you talk...?
I've never seen you talking.. " She said, still smiling, I rolled my eyes to heaven suddenly
wishing only if I had allowed this parrot to die in the plane. She wasn't even intimidated.
I shaked my head and continued walking..
She followed me, still chattering... "You know...
Many people in the Academy call you cold blooded... They say you're as cold as Ice.
They say you're emotionless...
But deep down.. I always felt that you were a kind person... You were never cold... You proved
that today by saving my life and I'm going to save yours as well...
I almost laughed...She could barely take care of herself... How would she save me...?
After trekking for more than 4 hours... I checked my wristwatch... It was already 6pm... It was
obvious that I My companion was already tired... She started talking again...
"Aren't you tired.. "
I didn't answer.
"I'm tired... "
I didn't answer
"Can't we rest a bit..We still have loads and loads of time to use"
I still gave her no reply.
"Ugh... My legs are hurting... "
I didn't answer.
"I feel like I'm gonna die from leg pains... "

Then I stopped abruptly... I could hear her laughing softly.

Without uttering a word, I sat down under a tree nearby giving her a bad look...

She gave me a funny face.. Like that of a five year old... I almost laughed.

She sat opposite me... Opened her bag and started eating some food.

Seeing her eating reminded me of my hunger... I opened my bag as well and started eating as well.

Soon the parrot opposite me started her talks again....

"You know... Everyone was given a different map, " she said.

I looked at her with a puzzled expression...

"Yes Angel... We weren't allowed to walk through the same path.

When I landed... Two other guys landed with me and all our maps was different

There are almost Twenty ways to reach this so-called building... "

I stretched out my hand in a gesture for her to pass over her map which she eagerly did....

She was right... our maps were totally different.. I had been wondering how come I didn't see any of the others from the academy except the parrot behind me...so they all passed different ways.

Deep down I knew the reason why the academy did that....

Those tricky evil teachers wanted everyone to be "ON YOUR OWN"

You face your challenges together with no one being able to help the other... We won't meet until we reach the building.

This was like "SURVIVAL FOR THE FITTEST"

I looked up to the parrot in front of me and wondered why she decided to follow me.

Like she was reading my mind... She answered my question.... "You must be wondering why I'm following you...

Well I have just one reason" she said and smiled.

"What reason? " I asked.

Normally for the first time "I know I'm not going to survive this...

I know I'm going to die but I don't want to die without leaving a message..."

I looked suspiciously at her for a few minutes... She smiled at me and removed her blouse... I looked away but she said laughing.

"See you... I'm not a lesbian...i want to show you something very important "

I looked at her naked chest and saw a peculiar tattoo imprinted on her two breasts....

I continued staring and it seemed like her tattoos were moving... I became confused.

"Your tattoos move...? " I asked.. I'm a little bit confused.

"They aren't tattoos... They are my dark side.."

"Dark side....?

What do you mean by that...? " I asked as my curiosity was already gaining more control over me.

She smiled again... And continued.

"I was born a twin... I had a sister. We were born by a powerful oracle of the Gods...

We were to fulfill a particular mission in the Forest.

This forest was known to accumulate some dark forces that are ranging to destroy the world.

Our mission was to conquer these dark forces which dwell in the cave of blood ruled by the queen of death and destruction....

Chapter Eight

In order to accomplish these... My twin sister was killed at the age of 19 and her spirit was imprinted in me... She's my dark side...
she's evil... she's powerful.. she's mighty
Only her in my body can conquer these forces.
But there was a problem... No one knew the exact location of the forest and my assignment was to find out where it was located and perform my duties... Take the green lamp which gives the queen power and return to my temple.
After lots and lots of research... I found out that some special world assassins go to a peculiar Forest and return powerful... The Forest claims the lives of the others as a sacrifice and releases only FOUR people and bestows them with an evil source of power that makes them invulnerable and abnormally strong.
I later discovered that it was the forest I was looking for.
So I managed to gain admission.... I looked into your heart and saw that you had a pure heart filled with revenge against someone who had hurt you
So I picked you for my Mission... You're my companion and you also made an attempt to save my life on the plane...
"I didn't make an attempt.. " I interrupted
"I saved your life, " I said.
She wanted to continue talking but I raised my hand..
"Enough of your nonsense...
Wear your clothes... I'm so tired of your bed night stories... Folktales meant for two year olds....
I don't believe any of that nonsense... You've been filled up with Religion Fanatics...
I don't know whether you're an oracle or not nor do I know how you came about that moving tattoo you call your dark side or whatever but I'm not interested in your mission.
I'm not on a mission to capture evil spirits or chase demons...
I'm a trained assassin facing her last exercise... Don't ruin it with your madness.
Get up....
Let's continue our journey.."
I thought she was going to argue but she surprisingly stood up without complaint and said,
"Seeing is believing, Angel.
Out of the fifteen people in this forest... you're the only one I'm going to rescue... you're the only one that's going to come out alive...
The main reason why I'm following you is because I'm not going to give the dark realm a chance to penetrate into your soul....
The others who get possessed aren't going to leave this place alive... Once I capture the green lamp... They will all die and turn to ashes except you
I'm going to protec... "
I didn't allow her to finish... I hissed and continued walking.
I wasn't in the mood to be brainwashed by someone like her.
We both continued walking until we reached a cave... The map shows that I will have to enter the cave to reach the building.
As we made it to enter, I heard Fiona whisper in Latin.

Nós Christi defenete

Malum ne fugat

Domine sospitate

Hoc sepulcrum caelo

Ne peturbetur

It translates...

Christ protects us...

Lord Above.. Keep us safe.. We beseech you... We leave this cave to heaven..May it never be disturbed, may the evil never escape.

Beyond this cave lies the workings of Satan... The will of the Devil.

I seal this passage against the Serpent of Eden, least Mankind be damned forever....

The moment she said these words...a great wind started blowing rapidly and I felt a chill running down my spine.

It was the beginning of a great Horror.

"Why are you trying to scare me..." I said angrily.

"I'm not scaring you " she replied looking innocently.

"At least.. Assassins don't get scared easily" it was obvious she was taunting me.

I hissed angrily at her and went into the cave...

She followed me inside, everything was dark and seemed ordinary.

I almost laughed and insulted her,I thought this was the cave she called the Cave of blood where the queen of death and destruction rules in the forest of Excalibur...

Mtcheeeew... The fool that has been brainwashed with rubbish...

I wasn't just in the mood to argue nonsensical topics with her.

The entrance of the cave was bright due to the light coming from outside...

We began our journey until we reached a particular point where everything was dark..

I switched on my disposable lamp ...She did the same as well everything was damn quiet..No creaking..No sound.

Nothing…Only our footsteps... The sounds of our boots touching the ground was audible... And the sounds of our breathing,even Fiona stopped chattering... She was quiet as well... For once, I wished she talked.. At least.

Having a voice around me was better than this abnormal quietness.

It made me uneasy and made me have a feeling of unrest.

Like she heard my inner thoughts.. She whispered.

"This quietness is odd..Something is lurking around...I feel like I'm being watched.. "

I turned around and Said..."Do you have to say that...? "

"Say what...? " she replied.

"Do you have to say you feel like something is watching us.."

"Well.. It was just my feeling and I... "

"Shut up.. " I interrupted

"Shut the fuck up... It's your feeling so keep it to yourself...You don't have to voice it out.. "

The truth was that I also had a feeling of being watched as well but having her confirm it made me more scared.

"You're mean...." Fiona muttered.

"So mean..." she repeated

I smiled to myself and pretended not to hear...We continued walking in silence then suddenly I started hearing a distant sound like something was dropping with a drop on the ground...
I was hearing " ta.. ta... ta..."
"What the fuck is dropping..?" I asked.
"Whatever it is..." Fiona replied in an odd voice, we continued walking and the sound became clearer.
The more we neared the front...the more my heart was thudding.. I was so scared
My heart kept on telling Me that whatever was in front of me was dangerous...
Suddenly I felt a drop of liquid on my head and another on my arm... Another on my leg, I stopped and touched my head and looked at it.....BLOODDDDDD!!!!!
I moved away quickly and raised my lamp. What I saw almost paralyzed me...
Above me were three human heads hanging from the top.. With open glazed eyes filled with fear...I opened my mouth to scream but nothing came out.
It was the neck that was bleeding.
Something horrorful and scary had ripped off their necks from their body and had hung them...
"These were some of the people from the plane. They are from the academy... They got here earlier.." Fiona said.
"What or who did this...? " I asked.
"Whatever or whoever did it is nearby.... " Fiona replied and immediately she said this...I heard a THUD!!!!
I quickly shoved my lamp towards the direction of the sound.
What was happening was too scary to say
I saw three headless bodies walking towards us,It was obviously the bodies of the dead people
The eyes on the head started moving left....right...right..left.
Then suddenly the mouth opened and made a terrifying sound...it sounded deep and croaky.
"Arrrrrrrrrrrrrggggggggg!!! " the head said with blackish blood dripping from the mouth,the eyes became black... The tongues became fangs.. Long like a snake's, like magic the bodies walked to the heads and carried them and carried them on their body....
"FIONAAAAAAAAAA..." I screamed
"RUNNNNNNNNNNNNN" I said and turned to run, she followed me and we turned left.. It was another long corridor... We started running together... My heart was pounding... It was so horrible... It was like a bad dream...
The bodies were resurrecting as demons... Blood thirsty demon..I was so scared.
I ran like a hare with Fiona on my heels.. These creatures were pursuing us hotly....
We kept hearing their scary sounds vibrating through the cave.
"Arrrggg.. Arrggg.. Arrggg..!!!!!!"
As we were running. We suddenly reached a dead end. All that remained was a wall... There was no place to run to... There was no way to escape. I closed my eyes and swallowed saliva.
I cleaned my sweat from my forehead and
I removed my guns..I held one in my right hand...the other in my left...stretched it and started shooting the approaching creatures... It only enraged them.
I started shaking...I looked back and saw Fiona looking calm.
"DO SOMETHING!!!! " I screamed.
She took a deep breath and said,"We have only one chance.. " she said calmly.

Chapter Nine

"WHAT'S THAT. ?" I screamed.
"We bring forth my dark side..My twin...."
"DO WHATEVER YOU CAN..
DO ANY FUCKING THING I DON'T CARE......"
"Cut me... " she said
"what...? " I asked.
**"I SAID FUCKING CUT THE DAMN SKIN... THESE THINGS ARE NEAR..AND IMMEDIATELY
I TRANSFORM... RUNNNNNNN**
MY DARK SIDE DOESN'T RECOGNIZE ANYONE ELSE
TILL I PASS OUT... DON'T MOVE NEAR Me.
CUT ME.. "she screamed.
I removed my Jack knife and moved near her,cut her arm and ran to the far curved end of the
cave and hid there and started watching from there.
The creatures were already in front of her ready to attack.
She looked slowly at her blood and fell onto her knees... A strange breeze started blowing
slowly and Fiona started floating....I opened my mouth in shock and amazement....She landed
and looked at my side and I saw that she was naked with black eyes and long nails.
She looked the same just that there wasn't any tattoo on her breast.
She was about to move near me until one of the creatures made it for her....
With fury and anger she dug her black long fingernails into the creature's chest and removed the
heart... Threw it into her mouth and started chewing...
With black blood dripping down her chin... She made the second one...
They fought for a while and the creature managed to give her a big cut on her cheek and she
healed instantly.
It infuriated her dark side and she plunged her hand into its chest as well and ate it...
It also dropped dead.
After the work was completed... Fiona fell down as well and became unconscious. I didn't move
for a while but later crawled to her side...
Although she was still naked her tattoo was back in place....
I opened my bag... Removed a bottle of water and poured little on her face.
she opened her eyes slowly...weakly
"Are you okay...? " I asked.
she smiled a little and said weakly, "It takes a bit to recover...
Hope you weren't so alarmed. ?" she asked...Looking worried.
"I was... A bit "
"Do you now believe me. ?" she asked.
"A bit.. " I said
"Do you know what made those bodies
resurrect... " I asked.
"No..." She said
"But soon we will find out.."

As she was so weak.... I carried her on my back out of the corridor back to the main path we were following.
I got tired after a while but we saw a door in front made from rock I guessed.
After lots of stress... We opened it and walked in...
It was wide leading to another pathway.
I looked at my watch....it was already 11pm, I was tired and hungry so we decided to camp there and rest....
We closed the door and ate a bit then we laid down....
The tension of our earlier adventure was still in me...I was still looking at Fiona like she was a demon.
She noticed and laughed softly and asked
"What are you thinking about...? "
,"Can you die... ?" I asked.
"Yes..." she said
"what happens to your dark side...I asked
"It comes out and dominates my body destroying anything at sight, it remains like that unharmed.
"Can't it be destroyed...? " I asked.
"Maybe... Maybe not...I don't know...."
We remained silent for a while and then slept off.
As I was sleeping... The heavy door opened slowly and closed again,it opened wide and closed again,It kept on like this until I woke.. Fiona woke up as well...
The door kept on opening and closing and we saw no one.
We sat down in fear watching with horror as the door opened and closed...Is the door magical...?
Or was something pushing it..?
Something invisible..?
Now I really believed that the cave was
bewitched. It wasn't ordinary.
So this was how people got powers...
My dear readers... Don't envy powerful people...Most of them got their powers from evil sources....
I now understood the reason why most of the criminals tutored from my academy became almost impossible to get...
It was because they were backed by an evil power...
The power that takes some people's life to
preserve just a few and it was this power that Fiona was here to stop.
Now I'm having an adventure.
I was in the world of supernaturals... The world many believe doesn't exist
Well, This world was real,It's real and it exists...Just that only few knows it.
Praying deeply.. I hoped to survive all this to live to tell the story.
Suddenly Fiona stood up boldly and,"Whether it's a demon or anything...
I'm going to find out..."
Because I was scared of being left alone...

I quickly jumped up and followed her... Before another demonic stuff appears before me. As we got to the front of the door... We noticed that there was a green glow from afar...It was blinking.. Like it was inviting us Fiona opened her bag and removed a peculiar looking glass.
"What's that..? " I asked.
"It's an ancient glass made from Egypt... It
contains psychic powers and is able to know when the True lamp I want to get is....You know...this cave is dangerous... We mustn't make a mistake.
She brought forth the glass and showed it to the direction of the lamp but nothing happened.
"It's a set up, " she said.
"We aren't going...
Let's continue our journey.."
Then we walked down and down the cave from outside ..it seemed small... But the cave itself was a small village.
For two good days we wandered and wandered down the cave without encountering anything but on the third day.
A very strange thing occurred,I really can't remember how it happened but all I remembered was that we suddenly found
ourselves in a cold place filled with snow.
It was so cold... Like it was at its freezing point,I looked up and saw a particular picture... It was drawing me in.
"STOPPPPPP" I heard Fiona scream...
"IT'S THE QUEENNNNNNN... SHE'S PLAYING MIND GAMES WITH YOU...
DON'T LET HER CONQUER YOU... SHE'S CONTROLLING YOU."
But it was too late, I saw myself as a child again watching uncle Harry abuse me brutally....I started feeling the pain again...
I started experiencing anger... The rush of emotions..
I felt adrenaline pumping into my blood. I felt the rage.
I saw Mom and Dad dying
I saw how Uncle Harry said "I killed your parents..."
It kept on echoing in my head.
"I killed your parents..I killed them... "
I looked and saw Fiona but she was fading
away... I was hearing her screaming...
"Stopppppppp....Stopppppppp..."
Slowly she transformed into Uncle Harry...
I saw her as him...I smiled wickedly and said,"I've always wanted to kill you.. Uncle Harry..."
"Stop Angel... You're being manipulated... I'm not that uncle,she's making you see me as
him...You can control it...she wants us to kill ourselves"
"You killed my parents
Ruined my life...
Destroyed me
You killed Meggie...
Oh Meggie...."

Chapter Ten

Fiona backed me... "You know I mustn't
bleed Angel....please don't bring forth my dark side"
"I'm going to make you suffer uncle Harry... " I said, looking so evil.
I brought out my Jack knife and moved swiftly near her to cut her but she avoided me
quickly...."Come back to me... Angel..
This is not you.. ' I heard her saying but I
I couldn't control myself...I kept on attacking her blindly and she kept on trying her best not to
get cut... Because once she
sees her blood...Her dark side becomes unleashed.
All of a moment, I saw Meggie walking towards me...
She was wearing her familiar green gown
I stopped my tracks and faced her.
"Meg... Meggie...
Is that you..? " I asked.
"Yes my love...
It's me.."
"I thought you were dead..."
"I came back for you... Come to me my love...Come to me"
I started moving towards her...Fiona was
screaming trying to stop me but I wasn't even normal.
"YOU'RE BEING MANIPULATED...
WHATEVER YOU SEE... WHATEVER YOU FEEL ISN'T REAL... IT'S A MIND TRICK DON'T
GO THERE...IT'S DANGEROUS!!! ANGEL... STOP IT!!!! "
I guessed she eventually managed to hit my head with something heavy,Instantly I passed out.
When I woke up....I felt horrible especially when Fiona recounted all the madness I
performed..."I'm sorry.. " I said.
She smiled and said.."Don't be.
you just witnessed the power of the green lamp and the evil it unleashes...
It needs to be kept away from the world"
"But how come you weren't affected by the mind tricks.. ?" I asked.
"See Angel...
I was brought up by an oracle....
I spent hours disciplining myself... Spent hours meditating...
My mind can't be easily controlled"
"So how are we going to get this green lamp of yours..? " I asked...
I was suddenly tired of everything... I wanted it to end on time.
Fiona brought out the strange mirror and it shone green brightly...
It was so bright that my eyes hurt from the
reflection.
"Soon... " She said smiling
"We are near it."

We continued walking in this cave for another two days...my food supply was almost finished...I prayed for everything to stop...One night...As we slept peacefully.

An odd smell woke me up... I felt something dropping on my skin.

I opened my eyes and saw that monster standing over me... Like the two we killed at the cave entrance

There were over 50 in the place where we slept...Blood was stinking everywhere... They were all looking scary.

Imagine waking up to see such a creature over you at night... What will you do ?

As for me, I freaked Out and shouted

"MUMMMYYYYYYYYYYYY!!!!!!!!"

Fiona woke up instantly and was equally

surprised... Before we were attacked... I

quickly cut her leg... She looked at her blood and transformed again into a blood thirst animal...I assisted her this time... But kept a great distance between us...

In thirty minutes.. The creatures were all dead but the scary part was that Fiona, the dark one, refused to go back as usual...

it kept on looking for more blood...

I hid behind a rock, shaking severely....

What if Fiona's dark side kills me...

I started having strange thoughts when I saw a particular green light from a distance...It looked liked a small fountain with green like water pouring out from it

Beside it was a very small green vial...

It was empty...Instantly my brain clicked.

'The Green Lamp..."

But then I became confused...what should I do..?

"Should I wait till Fiona transforms...I should go and carry the vial..."

"What if I carry the vial and something bad happens to me?.." I thought.

"Or what if I needed to recite some strange things before I took it..."

"What if I turned into a rock or something.."

All these thoughts were running around my head.

In the end, I decided to be strong... Since Fiona was still in her bad form.

I stood up and ran for the vial...but to my surprise... The more I ran... The more the vial went farther... I ran with all my strength but it was like I was running on a spot...

I tried to stop but couldn't stop... I continued running.

Then I saw it.... It was like a serpent... Green in color...I remembered Fiona's first words when we were entering the cave.

"THE SERPENT OF EDEN!!!!

THE WORKINGS OF SATAN

"THE WILL OF THE DEVIL "

Those words kept echoing in my skull

SERPENT... SATAN.. DEVIL... WILL.. WORKS.

It became louder...

Now I was hearing it in Latin...

It was in a whisper form...but it was loud

I know it's confusing...
A loud whisper... But come to think of it, close your eyes... Imagine it.
Hear the words... Hear it,It's coming soft. Yet it's hard,It's resounding... It's vibrating
It's scary
"MALUM NE FUGAT ...!!!!!
DOMINE SOSPITATE
HOC SEPULCRUM CAELO...!!!!! "

May it never be disturbed
May it never be disturbed
May it neverrrrrr be disturbeddddddd!!!! "
I started screaming... I started turning...
The greenish stuff was really powerful and strange.It was controlling my mind.
Filling it with fear.. With horror...I started turning on a spot.. Screaming loudly.
The greenish stuff rose up like flames.It was odd but strangely beautiful like a dark evil beauty.
I was scared and fascinated...
It was drawing me in... I wanted to touch it
Feel it....Twirl it in my fingers, I wanted to know how it felt..I moved nearer... Near the liquid,then
a very commanding tone said.
"STOP!
IT'S YOUR DEATH"
Like magic, the stuff lost it powers over me
I shaked from head to toe and my eyes and head cleared.
I turned and looked back and saw Fiona and another person that looked so much like her, Like I
saw two people staring at me.
Two Fionas...
I was scared... I moved back slowly
"Fiona....?" I called.
"Fiona, I'm seeing two of you....
Is it my eyes or that greenish stuff.. Is the demon affecting my eyes...?
I'm seeing you presently as two persons...
Tell Me I'm mad.
Tell Me that I've been possessed finally... Please tell me that something is wrong with me..."
One of the Fiona stepped forward and said..."Calm down baby...
It's not an illusion... Remember I told you that I was a twin.. And that my twin is my dark side...?
Remember...? "
"Yes... Yes... I do.
But she was killed right . She was killed to make her your dark side... Wasn't she? "
"Yes she was... Her soul was merged inside me..
She became my dark side..." Fiona replied.
"So who... who....who....is that? " I asked, pointing at the other one.
"That's her soul...? " Fiona said with a smile.
"Soul...? "
'But how come...? "

Chapter Eleven

Fiona smiled again.
"See Angel....There's a lot of things you're yet to understand about the supernatural......The supernatural world balances the natural world.
If the supernatural world is being tampered... Great harm will be done to the natural world,you see that greenish stuff curling... That we want to capture doesn't belong here... Humans are misusing it... It was stolen from its main place where it was used to do works of the supernatural and was being guarded by the Oracle... Passed from generation to generation
when misused... It affects all humans.
But it can't be taken anyhow...It's powerful..It's scary....It's strong...Way too strong to be played with.
You shouldn't be seeing my twin's soul but the power is opening your eyes to spiritual things...Do you know that every one of us is being affected by the power.
My twin left my body so as to be able to join powers with me to capture it.
You've done so well Angel... This is where you step back... Move to a safe distance and watch us,watch us save humanity.
I did as I was instructed, moved to a safe distance to watch the drama going on... It looked like a movie...I just couldn't believe it.
Was this real or was I day dreaming ...?
It was so scary....Fiona had said earlier
"Angel...The name is El Sagrido...
It means "The devil's blood "
It deals with the mind... Attacks and feeds off a vulnerable mind like yours... A soft open mind...To conquer this...your mind must be closed.
It takes great discipline.. meditation and training to do this... you can't do it ....So stay far..
Where it won't be able to reach your mind.
As for us, We will prevent it from penetrating our minds.It's a battle of the mind...."
From where I stood, I watched the two of them remove a rosary like bead from their pockets...
Just that the beads were bigger.
It looked like beads used by monks
But it was made from Gold... Pure Gold.
They sat down like people in a great meditation.
I hope you remember how monks sit with a straight back and folded legs.... Then they closed their eyes and raised the beads up with the right hand towards the direction of the stuff.
The stuff rose up in that beautiful attractive form of before that attracted me but this time it had no effect on me.
It rose like smoke... Curling and rolling... Just that its color was green, not white...
it started spreading around the twins. moving like a snake...
It started moving around them... Then went through the middle of them... But it seemed that it wasn't achieving its goal.
It changed approach
It rose up in a scary manner and started penetrating into the twins body. It would enter from the front in four different places and come out back from the other side

It was swift and quick.
I could see that the twin didn't move at all... They were just rigid.
Then all of a sudden they started floating with the green stuff... I could see that they were already gaining the upper hand.
They joined hands together and started speaking strange words I didn't understand
Soon the green stuff started rolling down until it became a small green stone. It was so small... Smaller than my baby finger.
I opened my mouth in shock....
Fiona's twin disappeared immediately, she was captured and Fiona fell down... Weak and tired.
I ran to her side and carried her up
she looked at me with blurry eyes and said
"it is done...."
I smiled and hugged her...I didn't know when I started sobbing.
She hugged me back and said.
"Now to the building...No need for maps....
Just close your eyes..."
I closed my eyes and when I opened it...i was In the building.
The four tubes were small containers filled with the greenish stuff.
I saw them at the four corners of the room
Fiona Explained to me "The four students that make it here every three.. three years drink this stuff and it makes them strong and abnormally powerful.
The source provides it in exchange for taking the lives of their mates...
But now that I have seized the main source... These things are meaningless but poisonous... Anyone that drinks it will melt instantly.
Just then... Seven others from the academy arrived in the building and started fighting for a tube... I tried to warn them but Fiona stopped me...
"They won't listen.." she said.
"Their souls have been corrupted and possessed.
They have been filled with thirst for blood and power,the forest has affected them, let them be... they are beyond redemption.
They are meant to die "
They killed themselves until it reminded the four and as soon as they drank it.
They dropped dead....
In that way, I was saved by Fiona . It was one of the greatest adventures of my life.
Fiona took me to a place where I was going to have to wait for the academy's helicopter as it was written on the building's wall with the empty case of the tube as a proof that I drank it
I also took an empty tube with Me even though I didn't take it.
As soon as we heard the sound of the helicopter approaching... Fiona said.
"My love....I have to go to the place I belong to,knowing you is one of the best things ever.
Our path will never cross again but I will never forget you,I will always pray and meditate on your behalf.
The world is a dangerous place,I wish you the best of luck...Goodbye..."
We hugged like sisters...
I cried like a baby and I felt her crying as well.

"Goodbye Fiona... "
"Goodbye Angel.. "
"I love you Fiona..."
"I love you Angel.. "

We hugged again and she disappeared..
I never saw her again.
I returned to the academy as the only survivor and graduated with Justin.
Then I took a plane to Canada with Justin by my side.

TIME TO REVENGE
I left Nigeria,a small timid scared heart broken girl... I left Nigeria with fear and pains,I left
Nigeria with anxiety....I left my motherland filled with depression and anger.
But I'M BACK!!!!!!
SANDRA IS BACK!!!!!

I was laughing to myself as we landed in
Airport...
Uncle Harry is in soup... This is what we call, "KARMA" He wouldn't know what hit him.
I'm one hundred percent sure that anytime my name crosses his mind... He would just wave me
off saying that he has gotten rid of me... It's either I'm dead or suffering bitterly somewhere...I
knew that those were his evil thoughts.
But he's wrong, After over 8 years, I'm back for **Revenge**
My people, do you know how sweet revenge is especially when the victim doesn't see it
coming...?
It would just hit them... "BANG!!!! " from any angle.
The shock, The thrill, The excitement was
everything that filled my soul.
Justin Noticed it but kept quiet.....
We already had a superb sweet plan....
This plan of ours was a great plan....
The plan that I'll used to destroy uncle Harry,
"You know... I've never been to Canada before"
Justin said to me as we entered the room we booked for in a big 5 Star Hotel...
"Do you like Canada...?" I asked with a big smile on my face.
"Hmmmmmm... ' he said, giving me a fake serious look.
"I'm still thinking about it... I'm yet to make up my mind " he replied.
"Hey " Justin said pretending to be angry
"Whatever you call that English you speak... Don't say it to me again... You know I don't
understand it...That Language is so complex to understand..
"I shrugged nonchalantly...
"Well, Justin... There are some things you can't know...Because you understand several
languages doesn't mean you must understand my language.

Chapter Twelve

Not everybody can speak it fluently... That's the uniqueness of it and that's why I love it....."I said with a tone of finality.
Justin gave me a mischievous smile and moved slowly towards me. I backed away with a smile too... I knew what he wanted to do.
"So Angel...what about me...
Ain't I unique as well.. " he drawled as he neared me... I moved back with a shy face.
"Actually Justin.. You're emmmm... You're the best of your kind... You're cool..."
He was already in front of me... He captured my face gently in between his hands and kissed me on my forehead.
"Just cool...? " he asked.
"Am I just cool...? " he asked again.
"Well you're romantic too.. " I said with a big smile.
"You forgot, I'm hot... I've got a hot face..
Hot body... Hot smile... I'm hot, baby " he said, kissing my lips this time.
I chuckled softly.
"Yeah.. Yeah... You're hot Justin... My love is hot"
Then I wrapped my arms around his neck and kissed him passionately.
I was already getting more attached to Justin...The more time I spent with him... The more he gained my trust.
Somehow my body was already responding to his touch... Although we avoided sex because I was yet to recover finally.
The trauma and pains of the abuse I faced was yet to fade finally so we still needed more time and Justin was ready to wait all through and give it what it takes.
We romanced a lot and did a lot of touchings....Somehow I pitied Justin because whenever we get intimate...I always feel his dick rising.. I feel it so hard between his legs but I'm so grateful for
his self control although I've caught him
masturbating countless times.
Two weeks later, Justin walked into my dad's company, now Uncle Harry's company as Mr Maximiliano, a rich foreign investor who wanted to invest millions in his company.
He arrived.
We planned it well....He arrived in all pomp and show.
He had bought almost 45 percent of the
company's share.. He was a major shareholder.
My evil uncle welcomed him with all respect and humility...
No one would imagine him capable of doing such evil.
Back in the hotel where I stayed, I started doing some research...
The house my parents built with their sweat had been put up for sale.
The first thing I did with the raw cash I brought back from the Academy was to buy that house back anonymously... I didn't want him suspecting anything...so I just bought it and made the estate agent believe that I was a foreigner soon coming

to Canada to stay and I needed a house for my family and I.
The man bought my lie and I bought the house under Justin's name....
The next thing I did was finding Meggie's parents and family.
To my despair... I found them in big suffering...The mother kept blaming herself... Saying she was responsible for her daughter's death...She kept on saying with tears rolling down her cheeks.
"Meg said," No , the first time I introduced this man to her,she said she wasn't interested... she said she didn't like him... but I forced her... Because of my greed... My selfishness... I saw money and forgot
my position as a mother... I didn't care about her feelings...I made her marry him.
Now the poverty I'm avoiding is back to me fully,I lost my daughter again... I will never forgive myself " she said and burst into tears again
It was a lesson though.. A lesson to every youth out there.
One day, you're gonna be a parent, some are even parents already.
Please and Please, No matter the situation you might be passing through... Never allow money to be your priority for your Children's spouse.
Never force them to marry someone they don't want to,never allow greed overshadow your parental responsibilities...your children's happiness should always come first.
After a while of talking and counseling them, I said.
"Actually, Meggie is someone I love so much she's someone that did what no one else has done before.
I'm alive and standing in front of you now
because of her and forever will I be grateful to her.
As from today, poverty is no more In your family"
I bought them a house... Gave them enough money and kept in touch with the last born who was a graduate from the University.... To my joy, he studied Accounting... Knew a lot about business,
I started buying shares in my father's company under his name.
I planned with Justin to hand over the company to him after everything had happened.
Next,
I started doing research about Uncle Harry's private life.
To my anger, I found out that he was doing well,he had remarried with four kids.. three girls and one boy.
After more research, I noticed that the first born was around 10, it was obvious that he was cheating on Meggie by the time he had her
One clue led to another and I found out that she was Meggie's best friend.
Wow... So uncle Harry was sleeping with his wife's friend all these while and that one had a secret child for him.
I decided to start my revenge with her for Meggie and For me as well.
I kidnapped her one sunny afternoon.. drugged her and brought her into my parent's house.
I had redecorated a special room for my works
I placed her into a glass like a cube.. It was like a standing coffin or like a standing big fridge.
Just that it was made of glass and was so

transparent... The top had a circular small hole which I connected to a particular long pipe that pumps water into...
I placed a small hearing instrument in her hair so that when she becomes conscious she would hear whatever I've got to say from within the glass.
After locking her up...
I set my cameras on her face and changed into black clothes.
I placed the camera till the extent that the only place you can see is my chest downward..Nothing else.
Then I went back to my system and started my hacking work,I hacked into every available channel....Everything.
in five minutes I did it and what everybody was watching at home was the terror I was about to do.
The only people who didn't watch were those who had no electricity and those playing DVD compact disc ...Homes, Shops, Supermarkets,Hotels, Hospitals, Bars, even Banks and offices tuned to any TV channels were suddenly seeing me.
All over the country, people were watching me.Soon my victim started becoming conscious.
"Hi dear... " I said.
she obviously heard as she turned her head into my direction... She looked confused...
"I know you're wondering who I am... "
"I'm Angel but I prefer you calling me Black Angel.
Here.. Right in this room, all I perform is jungle Justice.
This room is my court... I'm the judge, I'm the lawyer, I'm the law.
You don't need to do anything, just relax and receive your punishment.
I wonder why you stole your friend's husband,had a beautiful girl for him.
Not only that, twelve years ago ,back in the University, you killed two innocent people.... Due to a cultist clash... Babe.. You were a cultist..." I said and burst into laughter.
"Ten years ago, you drowned your step sister's five year old kid in the swimming pool and lied that the girl fell into it ....
Why did you do that...? " I whispered... "You shouldn't have?"
I could see her shaking...
I turned to the camera and faced my audience...They couldn't see me... But they saw my body.
"This lady deserves to die... Doesn't she? "
I asked...
"Well as the judge,
I sentence you to death by drowning as well,Not just drowning.... Freezing as well... "
She started beating the glass pleading, crying as I turned the switch on as ice cold water gushed down onto her head into the glass...
It was very cold water... The temperature
started dropping...Soon it reached her waist,then her neck...Then it covered her up.
She started struggling... Started screaming...It was so horrific... So gruesome,and 65% of the country even the president watched her die.
Overnight, I became a super star, everyone was busy talking about me on social media, In offices, schools,and gatherings.
I was always the topic of discussion.

Chapter Thirteen

Everyone was talking about the angel in black.
Some said I was delusional.... Some said I was a cold blooded killer...
Some said I was doing the right thing in the wrong way, While some said I was doing the right thing... The only way to overcome the ills of the society itself
is to be a very violent person.
A particular evening, I was in a supermarket buying things for myself when I heard some teenage girls discussing...
One said.." I want to be like Black Angel ?"
The other in a pink gown replied "Why? "
"I want to be able to kill my dad's step brother...He's a wicked man... Ever since my daddy had died,he seized all our properties and made us suffer in the last building that my dad built... It was the smallest building my dad had...We don't have much to eat again like before and I
I think he harasses my mum before giving us money.
Last week, I saw him forcefully kissing my mom behind the backyard.... I felt rage... I wanted to kill him.
I hated him with passion... My mother was
powerless... She was fighting him at first but the moment he said... "Do you want the money for your children's school fee or not...? "
Immediately my mom heard this... She became quiet and allowed him to continue...I really wanted to kill him " she said with tears pouring down her eyes... Her other friend hugged her tightly and started whispering sweet words into her ears.
I heard everything from where I stood and
followed the girl secretly home... I watched her house for two days non stop until I marked the uncle's face... He visited most evenings between 6pm till 8pm... He leaves and then visits the nearby bar and drinks from 8:30 till 10pm.
Half drunk.. He makes it home by 11pm
I noticed all his movements and mapped my way of kidnapping him.
One fateful Evening... I successfully took him without attracting a single person.. No one knew how I took him.
Then I took him straight away to my residence, to my courtroom
His own killing would be different... I placed him on a bed... And tied him securely with a strong belt.
I prepared a drip down and passed the needle into his veins but I didn't turn it on
I tied him very tight that he couldn't move a
finger.
Then I went to hack as usual... It was impossible to trace me because I turned on several GPS...No one knew my exact location.
Immediately I turned on, everyone already knew.
Even my neighbors living next door started screaming...
BLACK ANGEL IS BACK
BLACK ANGEL IS BACK

Only if they had known that I was performing my work in the next building.... (Laughter)
The camera didn't show my face as usual and I was dressed in all black.
On my front top
"BLACK ANGEL " was written boldly.
"Good evening my dear people,
Welcome to my humble court,
I remain your favorite ...Black Angel.
Tonight will be as horrorful as before...
Relax and grab a popcorn as I deal with my culprit.
Soon he started waking up... He was also
confused at first... But I guessed he noticed the room and his senses clicked.
Perhaps he watched my last show.... He started struggling madly,I laughed softly.
"Welcome to my court Mr Louis... I guessed you're a fan" I said and laughed again.
His expression showed total fear.... He was shivering.
"You recognized me already so no need for introductions....
But let me tell you the simple rules of my courtroom.
This is my COURT
I'm the Judge
I'm the Lawyer
I'm the Law....
You don't need to talk...You don't need to beg,Pleading isn't allowed and lies aren't tolerated.
Just relax and enjoy your verdict...
I've watched your every movement for the past weeks and I came up with some interesting
facts.
You killed your own step brother three years ago...it was you who did something funny to his car
brakes...
It made him lose control and that led to his
accident.
"True or false? "
He quickly nodded with tears pouring down his eyes.
Your brother survived the accident and was hospitalized but your greed couldn't be
satisfied...You went into his room and removed his life support machine... You removed the
oxygen and due to that... He died... Didn't he? "
He nodded again.
"You didn't stop at that... You bribed his lawyer with huge cash to lie that there wasn't any form
of written will...
Your brother wrote down a will... Didn't he?
He nodded again saying yes...
You didn't stop at that... After acquiring all the properties... You went ahead to torture his family.
You harassed your brother's widow sexually,threatening her with money for the children's
upkeep.
Yes or No?"
He nodded yes again...
I moved to his bed and whispered In my deadly voice.

"Why did you do that...?
You shouldn't have..."
He was already begging for mercy...crying bitterly,I opened my briefcase.
Removed some files and said....
"This states that you're handing over the
properties belonging to your step brother back to his family... Everything.. Not a single dime
remaining.
Sign it!!!"
He signed it without hesitation and handed it over to me. I showed the audience my paperwork
and smiled.
"If anyone tries to threaten the family again...You will end up in my court and I will decide your
fate... Trust Me... It won't be a good one.. " I warned the audience
Then I turned back gently to my captive... His face made me laugh.
"How does it feel to have poisons in your blood streams...? " I asked.
"Because that drip you're looking at is a very poisonous stuff meant for you alone "
His eyes widened in shock and terror.
He started begging me... Started promising to do anything.
"I'm so sorry Sir " I said in mock pity... Like I was really Sorry.
"Nobody leaves my court alive... Except me of course "
Then I turned on the drip set...Soon he started foaming In the mouth and was dead in a matter
of minutes.
At first Justin was angry about the change of plans... Why will you suddenly want to start killing
other people that needed jungle justice?
But then, I persuaded him... I made him
understand that with what I just did... he will never suspect me.
He will never think I'm back for revenge
He will be suspecting a random attack since I've already attacked someone not related to him.
He won't bother escaping from the country and that would buy Justin enough time to
accumulate all the needed to overthrow him.We noticed that even most of the staff doesn't like
him. It would be easier to win them over.
Justin agreed and maintained a very close relationship with my uncle.
Especially after his wife's death....he stood by him and offered him support and assistance with
all these, my uncle trusted him wholeheartedly....
Unknown to him that the devil was his best friend.
I continued taking important personnel doing wrong in society and killing them. I became viral.
All over the country...even outside.. I was known to be funny enough... Many started
appreciating my efforts especially that youth.
Many clothes were designed with "BLACK ANGEL" all over it.
My favorite saying was also used in clothes...handkerchiefs... Bags,It was always written in
black.

Chapter Fourteen

"YOU SHOULDN'T HAVE DONE THAT.."
It was used as captions on posts on instagram and facebook... Everywhere... I was everywhere people started using it to insult one another on the street.. You will hear them saying.
"I hope you end up in black Angel's court... "Some will say,
"You deserve the Black Angel "
Others will say,
"Black Angel's property.... "
Everywhere I went... I heard tales about me,many supported me while some were against me, But I didn't care... While Justin was fixing things up, I was serving people justice...
Any citizen that wasn't punished by the law gets punished by me soon. The crime rate dropped seriously but every law enforcement agency was looking for me up and down but I was well trained..I was untraceable.
All my plans became a success on the 12th of June.....
Justin did his part well... He succeeded in owning 52% of the company's shares by buying at a very high price from most shareholders...
It was so difficult but he did it...
Everything was bought in my name.
An Emergency major shareholders meeting was called for... Almost all the 45 major shareholders were present including Justin.
The Motion was to remove the present chairman, Mr Harry....due to charges like embezzlement and misuse of office power
It was a great shock for my uncle to see many people go against him...he felt betrayed... The hurt.. The pain.. But it was just the start although he was no longer a chairman... He was still a major shareholder.
He stood up from the main seat and sat down round the next chairs with anger... He looked at Justin with evil eyes but Justin didn't care Justin stood up and said.
"Let me introduce you to the real owner of all the shares... She's the new candidate for the post of the CEO only if you allow her to...Meet the only daughter of the first chairman and founder of this company,SANDRA SAMUEL!!!!!!!
The door opened and I walked in with flourish. 45 pairs of eyes strayed to me...I felt on top of the world.....Uncle Harry recognized me immediately...He stood up with shock and astonishment.... I almost burst into laughter....I didn't know when water filled my eyes...I saw my parents in my mind's eye looking at me from the end of the conference table.... They both held hands smiling.
at me....They looked so proud of me
YES... MOMMA....PAPA... I MADE YOU PROUD... I COLLECTED YOUR PROPERTY BACK BUT I HAVEN'T REVENGED YET... I JUST STARTED.
Still smiling.. I introduced myself as the long lost daughter of the former Ceo of this company... Most of them still recognized me and smiled at me.
"I've come back to take my dad's place.. I hope I'm welcome back..."

Everyone started clapping with happiness... They all encouraged me...i felt pure joy...i almost started crying again because I was already getting emotional, I learnt something from what happened....

"THE BEST WAY TO GET FULL REVENGE FROM YOUR ENEMY IS TO SUCCEED IN THEIR"

PRESENCE.....
I loved the shock on uncle Harry's face... The wonder...The regret... I loved it
After the meeting, I sat down on the CEO seat, turning the chair round and round.... After every shareholder has left... Uncle Harry and I left in the room...After a long silence.. He spoke, "I'm sorry Sandra... "
I pretended to look surprised ... "Sorry for what? "I asked...
"None of this was your fault... "
He looked confused,
I smiled and continued... I don't really remember.
what happened but I knew Meggie died in my hands and I ran out to call for help... In the process I was hit by a running car... When I gained consciousness... I had memory loss....
I didn't remember anything at first... Not even my name...The woman was a wealthy widow.. She took me abroad.. " I said, giving all the fake documents about me.... Including fake pictures of my accident... It was well planned.... I even tendered the doctor's note about my sickness...
The memory loss... Both in Nigeria and abroad.
"You can call them to be sure... " I said.
"After lots and lots of therapy... The only thing I remember was my name... And I also remembered Meggie dying In my arms telling me to pack up my things and run... I ran for help but I was hit... After that.. I don't remember anything at all.
I saw uncle Harry relaxing... "You don't remember anything..? " he asked.
"Yes...i don't... That's why I came back with my boyfriend...
I want you to tell me nothing else but the truth...
Then I will return the company to you...
I don't need the company.. All I needed is the truth...because it was discovered that I wasn't a virgin and I was still young... I don't remember having a boyfriend... I don't remember anything...
I don't even remember my parents.. How they died... When they died... I want you to come over to my house this evening with my cousins... Let's discuss over dinner... If you tell Me anything that sparks my memory and returns it... I will return it all to you.. And go back to my house, He fell for my lie.
By himself... He brought himself and his children to their death
I drugged them when they arrived at my parents residence... The room I used for my evil works was the same room where I was raped continuously... Uncle Harry's former room...I placed him inside a tight container and covered it tight leaving only a small space for air.
His three kids were placed in front of him...
Hands tied to the back.
When he opened his eyes... He was surprised, 'wh... what is happening here...? " he asked looking confused

Then he saw my clothes and the room and it hit him.

I WAS THE BLACK ANGEL

I KILLED HIS WIFE

I DIDN'T LOSE ANY MEMORIES

I TRICKED HIM

AND I WAS GOING TO KILL HIM

"Please don't touch those children... They are innocent... Please don't... Kill me instead.. I deserve to die"

I smiled softly.

"on one condition.. Confess your crimes " I said.

He turned to the small camera and said it all...From killing my parents to raping Me.. To Molesting me... To telling Meggie to kill me, he said it all... not leaving a little detail,

I was yet to go live then... No one saw that

part... I only recorded it and kept it for some purposes... I wanted to tender it in the court...because I wanted to get caught.. It was all my plans, exposing myself... Getting arrested...Taken to court... It was all my plans, that was why I said in the beginning of my story that everything was working according to my plans...

After he confessed it all... I kept the drive in my pocket and tuned the audience in... I was alive again but this time.. It was different,I showed everyone my full body but I turned my back to them...

Speaking loudly so that everyone would be able to hear me out ...I said.

"Today will be the last day you will be seeing me on your screen because I'm going to reveal myself "

I turned and faced the screen...."Today is my last operation... After this operation... nothing else matters, as long as I complete this... I'm happy"

I turned to uncle Harry and said,

"Uncle.... Do you remember this room... The first night of my 10th birthday

That unforgettable night

That unforgivable night

I was a little girl... Small and innocent you made me this,

YOU DID THIS TO ME

YOU MADE ME A BEAST!!!!!! "I screamed with anger, he started begging for mercy.

"Sandra....i beg you in the name of God

please spare my kid's lives... they are innocent " But my mind was made up..... I was adamant,he doesn't deserve to have children... he doesn't deserve mercy.. I remembered the beatings... The abuses... Both Meggie and I.

How he killed my parents and turned me to an orphan...I couldn't let his kids survive. who knows If one of them becomes a monster like him. Right in front of him... his first daughter... The one he had while cheating was brutally raped by a machine I bought... He kept on screaming with tears rolling down his face

"SANDRA PLEASE STOP!!!

SHE'S JUST ELEVEN!!! "

Chapter Fifteen

'"And I was just ten when you molested me," I replied with anger.
I killed the remaining two by hanging... it was short, brutal and painful... It was the most horrific killing I ever did.
I enjoyed every single moment of watching uncle Harry's life drain away...he kept begging and crying until I killed them all.
Then he became silent... His eyes lost any form of life... He looked lost and hopeless,
I liked it so much...seeing the man that made my life meaningless lying down so pitiful was a "Dream come true...
"For Meggie..For my parents and
For Me.... You're sentenced to death by cutting off your private part " I said with a tone of finality.
Uncle Harry started screaming "NOOOOOOOOOO....
PLEASEEEEEE "
I totally ignored him... sliced his dick into two...He started groaning In pain... Twisting and rolling..
It was a severe method of killing... He didn't quickly die.. Took him a lot of time and lots of pain.
He died and I waited patiently for the police to arrest me because I turned on my location making it easier to be traced.
I surrendered and here am I in the court **JUNE**
Telling you what brought me here
I still have the disc with me... Now I want you to judge me as the judge...
What do I really deserve...
Everywhere was silent, the whole courtroom was so silent that if a pin drops.. The sound would be heard clearly.
I looked around and saw that everyone had tears in their eyes... Even the judge looked a bit sad....I smiled and said.
"Didn't I warn you at the beginning of my story that you shouldn't cry for me...?
You all promised me not to cry... Now see you... See all of you...you're all crying"
Nobody uttered a statement for a while... Everyone was just looking.
I continued ....
"No one can really understand the pain I went through..
The torment... The sleepless nights... I was just a child!!!!.. I was a kid.
A small innocent kid... He turned me into this, if I had grown up innocent with my family and parents... I wouldn't be like this... I wouldn't be this hard... No one will be black Angel....perhaps I will be a doctor, or a lawyer or any nice profession...i won't be a cold blooded killer....
Most assassins you see out there... Most terrorist that ruin the nation was made by the people themselves.
Society made us... We didn't make it ourselves. Rape should be a very serious crime....Rapist should be killed brutally....
Children Abusers should be dealt with in a deadly manner, you don't know the scars left on kids who are abused sexually
The physical trauma,
The emotional trauma,

The mental trauma...
It's not easy....Sometimes I feel suffocated... I feel like killing him over and over again...
I loved the way he was crying for mercy...
Do you know the amount of times I also begged for mercy?
The times I cried out in pain... Saying
"Uncle please...Uncle please... Uncle it's paining me...
Uncle in the name of God... Have mercy... Do you know?
The times he hit me in my face...
The times he broke my teeth... Blood, saliva, and tears dripping down my chin to my clothes...
Imagine that nightmare... Just imagine it and tell Me that killing him and his family wasn't good enough...
Don't you know that his wickedness runs through his veins and blood?
What if one of his kids takes that trait and does the same thing to another innocent kid?
And the same thing repeats itself over and over again....I didn't want that... That's why I ruined his generation.
That's why I killed them all and I don't regret it, I'm not sober at all......
Even if I die right now....I'm dying in peace" I concluded.
The judge looked at me and said,
"Let me have the disc you recorded " I opened my shirt and removed it from where I kept it... No one knew that I had a disc with me.
It was played and uncle Harry's voice was heard as he confessed his crimes everything I said was true....
The judge asked...
"So what's going to happen to the company...? "
"I've transferred all my shares to Meggie's biological brother... He's the new CEO of the company "
" Where is Justin...? " he asked.
"I don't know... I haven't seen him in a while' 'I replied.
"Sandra... " The judge started...
" I wish I could help but my hands are tied... The law is tying my hands...
You shouldn't have killed his children...although you've stated your reasons for doing so... Yet, the law of the country doesn't justify your actions
They were just kids...11,9,and 5 years.... I can't let you go.
You still have to die for killing them...
I'm sorry Sandra " The judge had tears in his eyes and I saw that he treated me differently...
Even his voice had a tone of respect.
I smiled again... I had fulfilled my dreams...my plans.
Perhaps sexual harassment will reduce a bit perhaps men shall see the danger in abusing innocent females....
As I was led into the waiting police van with chains and handcuffs,I was happy... I was smiling, I had managed to touch people... I had managed to change a few people's hearts...
I saw cardboards raised high with different encouraging words like.

"I LOVE YOU ANGEL "

" YOU MIGHT BE BLACK ANGEL.. BUT YOUR SOUL ISN'T BLACK "

"I WILL NEVER FORGET YOU ANGEL... ALWAYS IN OUR HEART"
I didn't know when water filled my eyes and finally dropped down....
I might disappear from society but not from the people's hearts.... I will always remain loved.
Finally I passed my Message to the people
The same innocent kid that was abused today and forgotten might come back tomorrow as a
big terror to the community and even the nation.
That small 5 year old that was raped today and wasn't given justice might come back tomorrow
for the justice....

SAY NO TO RAPE
SAY NO TO SEXUAL HARASSMENT
SAY NO TO CHILDREN ABUSE

I entered the van gently... Even the police that were handling me roughly before started handling
me gently.. I almost laughed... Everyone was taking care of me like an egg
We started driving.... But suddenly we stopped...
I wondered what was happening but there wasn't time for explanations...the police beside me
removed a bunch of keys from his pocket and released me... He opened the back door and
said.
" Get down... "
I jumped down still looking puzzled
" We got orders from the higher authority to release you...You must leave the country at once...
Never to return...Change your name... Change your identity
And start all over again... Live a new life"
I opened my mouth in amazement...
" But how will I leave...? "
A familiar voice replied me from behind
"I'm taking you with me. "
I turned sharply and behold... I saw JUSTIN!!!!!
I didn't know what to do...I couldn't cry.. I couldn't laugh,I ran into his arms and hugged him
tightly... He patted me and said, "It's all over now babe...
The battle is over "
The policeman smiled at us... He saluted me and said, " You deserve an accolade
ma'am...You're a true heroine...I respect you "
He then closed the door and the whole entourage drove off leaving Justin and I in the middle of
the road.
He kissed me passionately and said,
"Where do you want to go babe? "
I felt free for the first time in my life... I laughed and kissed him back...
"Hmmmm... Anywhere... I want to see the snow.." I replied.

" Will you visit Kansas City? " he asked as he pulled my hands and walked me to a big black jeep nearby. I shrugged nonchalantly and said, "I don't care.. As long as I'm with you "
"I love you Angel... "
"I love you Justin... "
We kissed again and he turned on the ignition switch and drove off.

FIVE YEARS LATER.....
"Mrs Justin... " I heard
"That's me... " I said smiling and walked towards the woman as she handed me my test results
I didn't wait to reach the car before opening it... I wanted to check if I was right or wrong, so I opened it...
As I was reading it.. my vision blurred...i wanted to cry but I held it in
I was pregnant... I was really pregnant,so I placed my hand on my tummy... A little creature.. A beautiful alien is growing inside of me, I was going to be a mother....
I was so happy,as I picked up my phone to call Justin... I knew I was going to give birth to a girl and I'm going to name her Fiona Meggie.....
Justin and I lived in a big mansion in Poland....
He runs a small business that was booming and flourishing while I stayed at home. Soon we will have another small Justin roaming around the big house.Just the mere thought made me happy.
Justin picked up my call and said
"My Angel..."
"I love you Justin... " I said
"I love you more.. What's up? "
"Guess what? "
"What's that? " he said
"Say please... "
"Please Angel... I love you "
" I'm pregnant Justin... " I said and gave my usual soft laugh,he was happy hearing the news.
I WAS SO HAPPY, THAT WAS THE BEGINNING OF MY HAPPINESS,BOTH I AND JUSTIN LIVE HAPPILY AFTER WITH MY JUNIOR JUSTIN.

THE END